Mateo's Choice

Basic Discipleship for Children

Written by Anne Marie Gosnell
Illustrated by Emily Heinz

Mateo's Choice:
Basic Discipleship for Children

© 2018 Anne Marie Gosnell. All rights reserved. Permission is given to use said document in a home, school, church, or co-op setting. This document may not be transmitted in any other form or by any other means—electronic, mechanical, photocopying, recording, or otherwise—without prior written permission of Anne Marie Gosnell. Coloring pages may be copied for classroom lessons.

Illustrations by Emily Heinz

ISBN: 978-0-9981968-6-2 (print), 978-0-9981968-5-5 (epub)

Scripture quotations taken from the New American Standard Bible® (NASB), Copyright © 1960, 1962, 1963, 1968, 1971, 1972, 1973, 1975, 1977, 1995 by The Lockman Foundation. Used by permission. www.Lockman.org

Scriptures taken from the Holy Bible, New International Version®, NIV®. Copyright © 1973, 1978, 1984, 2011 by Biblica, Inc.™ Used by permission of Zondervan. All rights reserved worldwide. www.zondervan.com. The "NIV" and "New International Version" are trademarks registered in the United States Patent and Trademark Office by Biblica, Inc.™

ICB — Scripture taken from the International Children's Bible®. Copyright © 1986, 1988, 1999 by Thomas Nelson. Used by permission. All rights reserved.

Publishing and Design Services: MartinPublishingServices.com

From Anne Marie

This book is dedicated to those pastors and instructors who have taught me theology, ethics, and how to love Jesus:

Dr. Jack Layman,
Pastor Tony Qualkinbush, and
Dr. Chad Rickenbaker;

and to my parents,
who consistently took me to church.

From Emily

Now to the King eternal, immortal, invisible, the only God, be honor and glory forever and ever. Amen.

—1 Timothy 1:17

Thank you, Mom and Dad, for training me in the way I should go.

Dear Parents,

This book is written in a kid-friendly format. It explains what the Bible tells us about salvation, sin, and Christian living for kids.

Tips for using this book:

1. Read this book to your younger child. If your child can read, have them read the book to you.
2. Open a Bible and show your child where the verses are located. You might want to highlight them as well, especially if you are using the **Memory Chart** at the back of the book.
3. Be open to your child's questions as you go through the book. Your church might do some things differently. If you do not know the answer, that is all right. Tell your child that you will find the answer together.
4. *The Wordless Book* is a tool developed by Child Evangelism Fellowship. It consists of the colors Gold, Black, Red, White, Blue, and Green. Each color represents a part of the salvation process. As you read through *Mateo's Choice*, you will see these colors on the pages as he makes his choice about Jesus.
5. Mateo interacts with a bully in this book. Use this as an opportunity to have discussions with your child. While we are to have a heart of forgiveness, encourage your child to always tell you if they are being bullied.
6. At the end of this book, there is a chart to encourage you and your child to memorize simple Scriptures that explain the gospel and how to live a life that pleases God.

If your child chooses to follow Jesus, it is a big commitment. It is not a decision to take lightly. It is a commitment that will bring eternal life! May God bless your family!

Anne Marie Gosnell
www.futureflyingsaucers.com

Mateo thinks he wants to follow Jesus.

But he's not sure.

Following Jesus is a COMMITMENT. When you commit to follow Jesus, you become a Christian.

Reading this book can help Mateo, and you, learn what it means to be a Christian and to follow Jesus.

Commitment
A promise to be loyal, or faithful, to someone or something

Mateo knows he has sinned. Do you?

When you become a Christian...

You will want to tell God you are a sinner.

A sinner is anyone who thinks, says, or does anything that does not please God.

> "For all have sinned and
> FALL SHORT of the GLORY OF GOD."
> —Romans 3:23 (NIV)

Fall Short
Unable to be perfect like God

Glory of God
What God is like. He is forever, unchanging, and perfect.

Mateo feels sorry for the wrong things he has done. He wants to please God.

When you become a Christian...

You will want to ask God to FORGIVE you of your sins.

When you ask God to forgive you, you should try to stop doing sinful things with His help. This is called repentance.

> "From that time Jesus began to preach and say, 'Repent, for the kingdom of heaven is at hand.'"
> —Matthew 4:17 (NASB)

Forgive
To choose to forget that
someone did something to hurt you,
or did something wrong to you.
God wipes away our sins
each time He forgives;
our hearts become clean.

Mateo chooses to believe that Jesus can solve his sin problem.

When you become a Christian …

You will say you believe that Jesus is LORD.

To believe in Jesus means you trust Him and you choose to live your life by following Him.

> "If you declare with your mouth, 'Jesus is Lord,' and if you believe in your heart that God raised Jesus from death, then you will be saved. We believe with our hearts, and so we are made right with God. And we declare with our mouths to say that we believe, and so we are saved."
> —Romans 10:9-10 (ICB)

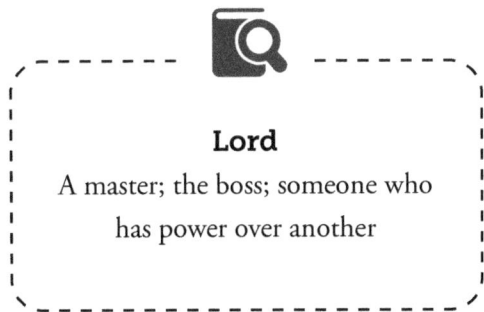

Lord
A master; the boss; someone who has power over another

Mateo wants everyone to know what Jesus did for him. He chooses to be baptized.

When you become a Christian...

You might choose to be baptized.

When you are baptized, it shows people that you used to be DEAD IN YOUR SINS, but now you are alive in Jesus.

Mateo is being baptized by immersion, which means he is dunked under the water.

> "Then those people who accepted what Peter said were baptized."
> —Acts 2:41a (ICB)

Dead in your sins
Separated from God

When you become a Christian...

You will want to obey Jesus.

To obey Jesus means He is in charge and now you do what He tells you to do. Jesus becomes your Lord.

If you want to obey Him, then you need to know what Jesus commands.

How can you and Mateo obey Jesus?

> "You are my friends if you
> do what I command you."
> —John 15:14 (ESV)

What does Jesus want you to do?

Jesus wants you to love God with all your heart.

> "Jesus answered, 'Love the Lord your God with all your heart, soul and mind.' This is the first and most important command."
> —Matthew 22:37-38 (ICB)

When you love God with all your heart, you will begin to love what God loves.

What does Jesus want you to do?

Jesus wants you to seek God's kingdom.

You seek God's kingdom when you choose to do what God wants instead of what you want. He rules your life.

You seek God's kingdom when you help others learn about what God has done for them through Jesus Christ.

> "The thing you should want most is God's kingdom and doing what God wants. Then all these other things you need will be given to you."
> —Matthew 6:33 (ICB)

What does Jesus want you to do?

Jesus wants you to PRAY.

God cares about what you think, feel, and do. You can tell Him anything. And if you listen, He will speak to you, too.

> "So when you pray, you should pray like this: 'Our Father in heaven, we pray that your name will always be kept HOLY.'"
> —Matthew 6:9 (ICB)

Pray
To talk to God

Holy
To be set apart

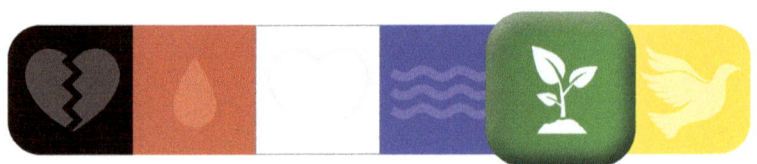

What does Jesus want you to do?

Jesus wants you to do the WORKS that He did.

While Jesus lived on earth He did many things.

We can learn about the works Jesus did by reading the BIBLE.

> "I tell you the truth. He who believes in me will do the same things that I do. He will do even greater things than these because I am going to the Father."
> —John 14:12 (ICB)

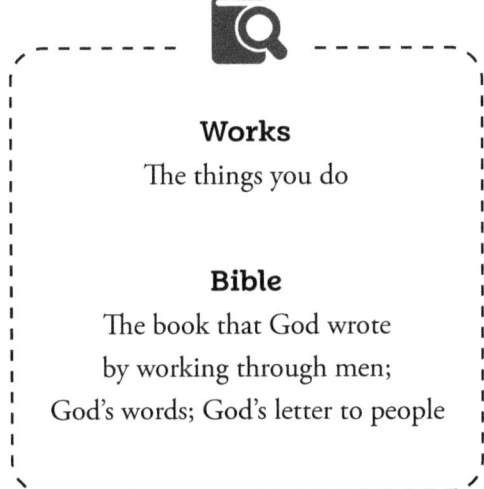

Works
The things you do

Bible
The book that God wrote by working through men; God's words; God's letter to people

What does Jesus want you to do?

There are times when it is hard to obey. Sometimes Mateo obeys, but he has a bad attitude.

Jesus wants you to obey your parents.

> "Children, obey your parents in all things. This pleases the Lord."
> —Colossians 3:20 (ICB)

Jesus also wants you to please Him with a good attitude.

What does Jesus want you to do?

Jesus wants you to treat people the way you like to be treated.

> "Do for other people the same things
> you want them to do for you."
> —Matthew 7:12 (ICB)

How do you want people to treat you?

How should you treat them?

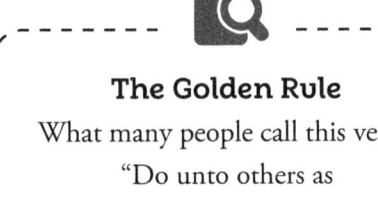

The Golden Rule
What many people call this verse:
"Do unto others as
you would have them do unto you."

What does Jesus want you to do?

Jesus wants you to love people the way He loves you.

Jesus loves you so much that He gave up His life so you could have eternal life.

> "I give you a new command:
> Love each other. You must love each other
> as I have loved you."
> —John 13:34 (ICB)

What is something you can give up to show love to another person?

What does Jesus want you to do?

Jesus wants you to love and pray for people who do not like you.

Has someone been mean to you?

Pray that they will choose to follow Jesus.

> "But I tell you, love your enemies. Pray for those who hurt you. If you do this, then you will be true sons of your Father in heaven. Your Father causes the sun to rise on good people and on bad people. Your Father sends rain to those who do good and to those who do wrong. If you love only the people who love you, then you will get no reward."
> —Matthew 5:44-46 (ICB)

What does Jesus want you to do?

Jesus wants you to FORGIVE people just as He forgives you.

> "Then Peter came to Jesus and asked, 'Lord, when my brother sins against me, how many times must I forgive him? Should I forgive him as many as 7 times?' Jesus answered, 'I tell you, you must forgive him more than 7 times. You must forgive him even if he does wrong to you seventy times seven.'"
> —Matthew 18:21-22 (ICB)

Do you need to forgive someone?

Forgive
To choose to forget that someone did something to hurt you, or did something wrong to you. Even though you might still feel angry or sad, you choose to forget it anyway.

What does Jesus want you to do?

Jesus wants you to ask God to send out workers.

> "Jesus said to his followers, 'There are many people to HARVEST, but there are only a few workers to help harvest them. God owns the harvest. Pray to Him that He will send more workers to help gather His harvest.'"
> —Matthew 9:37-38 (ICB)

God uses workers, or missionaries, to preach the GOSPEL. Jesus wants you to be a missionary in your house and town.

Harvest
People who have chosen to have Jesus as their Lord

Gospel
The good news of Jesus

What does Jesus want you to do?

Jesus wants you to preach the gospel and make followers, or DISCIPLES.

You can help bring in the harvest!

With whom can you share the gospel?

The gospel is the good news that Jesus saves us from our sins. When you share the gospel you tell others about God and Jesus.

> "So go and make followers of all people in the world. Baptize them in the name of the Father and the Son and the Holy Spirit. Teach them to obey everything that I have told you. You can be sure that I will be with you always. I will continue with you until the end of the world."
> —Matthew 28:19-20 (ICB)

Disciples
Those who follow Jesus.
Disciples are baptized and
they obey what Jesus commands.

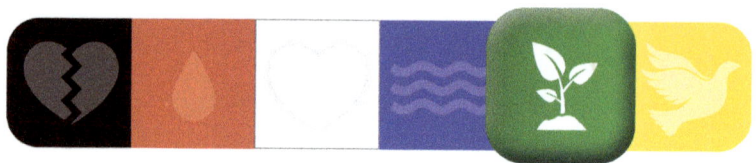

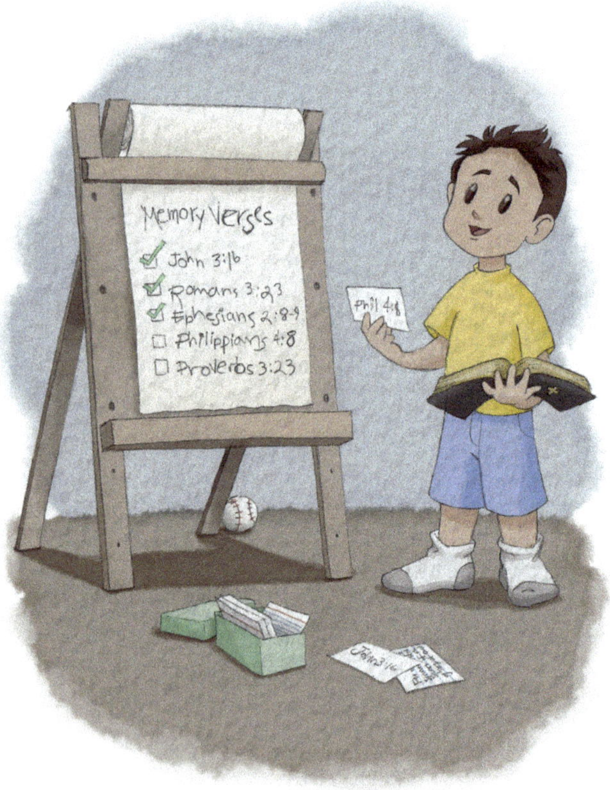
Memory Verses
John 3:16
Romans 3:23
Ephesians 2:8-9
Philippians 4:8
Proverbs 3:23
Phil 4:8
John 3:16

What does Jesus want you to do?

Jesus wants you to learn about and read the Bible.

Every word in the Bible is God's.

When you read the Bible, memorize some of the verses. This will help you to remember what Jesus said and what He wants you to do.

> "But He answered, 'It is written,
> "Man shall not live by bread alone, but by every
> word that comes from the mouth of God."'"
> —Matthew 4:4 (ESV)

What does Jesus want you to do?

Jesus wants you to remember His death and RESURRECTION.

You can remember this by being a part of the Lord's Supper at your local church.

The Lord's Supper is called Communion.

> "Then Jesus took some bread. He thanked God for it, broke it, and gave it to the APOSTLES. Then Jesus said, 'This bread is my body that I am giving for you. Do this to remember me.' In the same way, after supper, Jesus took the cup and said, 'This cup shows the new agreement that God makes with his people. This new agreement begins with my blood which is poured out for you.'"
> —Luke 22:19-20 (ICB)

Resurrection
The event when Jesus came back to life after being dead

Apostles
The men who saw Jesus face to face on the earth and were sent to share the message about Him with others

What does Jesus want you to do?

Jesus wants you to give.

You can give by taking a TITHE to your local church.

You can also give whenever you see someone is in need.

> "Your heart will be where your treasure is."
> —Matthew 6:21 (ICB)

Tithe
A gift of thanksgiving given to God;
equals one-tenth of earnings,
but you can always give more

If you believe in Jesus, then you have FAITH in Him.

It is your faith that pleases God and makes you RIGHTEOUS. But even your faith comes from God.

> "We have been made right with God because of our faith. So we have PEACE with God through our Lord Jesus Christ."
> —Romans 5:1 (ICB)

> "Without faith no one can please God. Anyone who comes to God must believe that He is real and that He rewards those who truly want to find him."
> —Hebrews 11:6 (ICB)

Mateo has faith in Jesus. Do you?

Faith
Trust in God. Sometimes we can have great faith, and sometimes it is as small as a mustard seed.

Righteous
Right with God

Peace
No conflict; no fighting with God

If you believe in Jesus, then the Holy Spirit lives in you.

When Jesus went back to Heaven, He sent the Holy Spirit to help people.

The Holy Spirit is God and is your helper.

The Holy Spirit tells you when you do wrong. He also helps you to do the things that Jesus wants you to do.

> "But you are not ruled by your sinful selves. You are ruled by the Spirit, if that Spirit of God really lives in you. But if anyone does not have the Spirit of Christ, then he does not belong to Christ."
> —Romans 8:9 (ICB)

Heaven
Jesus called it His Father's house.
He is preparing a place with no pain, suffering, or tears for those who believe in Him.

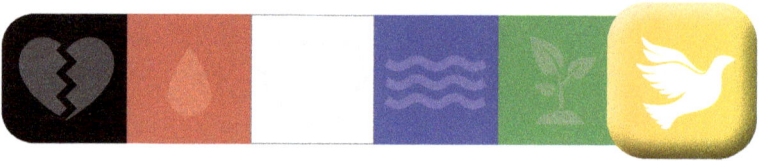

If you believe in Jesus, then your home is in heaven.

> "There are many rooms in my Father's house. I would not tell you this if it were not true. I am going there to prepare a place for you."
> —John 14:2 (ICB)

Mateo knows that when he dies he will be with Jesus in heaven.

> And he raised us up with Christ and gave us a seat with him in the heavens. He did this for those of us who are in Christ Jesus.
> —Ephesians 2:6 (ICB)

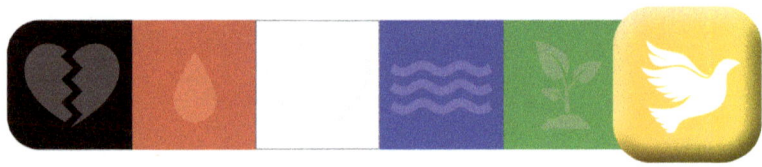

You might have questions about:

- God
- Jesus
- The Holy Spirit
- Baptism
- The Bible
- The Church
- Serving Jesus

Talk to a church teacher, your church leader, or your parents. They want to help you.

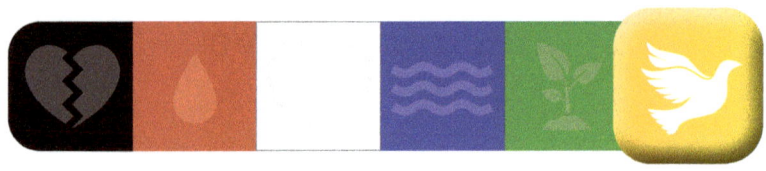

It is important for you to know if you are a Christian.

Answer these questions:

What did Jesus do for you?

> "For God loved the world in this way: He gave His One and Only Son, so that everyone who believes in Him will not perish but have eternal life."
> —John 3:16 (HCSB)

Jesus is the Son of God. He died on the cross and rose from the dead. He gave you eternal life!

How do you know that you will live forever with Jesus? Read the verse below for help.

> "Whoever has the Son has life. But the person who does not have the Son of God does not have life. I write this letter to you who believe in the Son of God. I write so that you will know that you have eternal life now."
> —1 John 5:12-13 (ICB)

Doing what Jesus tells you to do can be hard at times, but He will never leave you.

It is worth it.

You will be glad you have committed to follow Jesus!

> When a person is tempted and still continues strong, he should be happy. After he has proved his faith, God will reward him with life forever. God promised this to all people who love him.
> —Mark 1:17 (ICB)

Glossary

Apostles: The men who saw Jesus face to face on the earth and were sent to share the message about Him to others

Bible: The book that God wrote by working through men; God's words; God's letter to people

Commitment: A promise to be loyal, or faithful, to someone or something

Dead in your sins: Separated from God

Disciples: Those who follow Jesus. Disciples are baptized and they obey what Jesus commands.

Faith: Trust in God. Sometimes we can have great faith, and sometimes it is as small as a mustard seed.

Fall short: Unable to be perfect like God

Forgive: To choose to forget that someone did something to hurt you, or did something wrong to you. God wipes away our sins each time He forgives; our hearts become clean. Even though you might still feel angry or sad, you choose to forgive anyway.

Glory of God: What God is like. He is eternal, unchanging, and perfect.

Gospel: the good news of Jesus

Harvest: People who have chosen to have Jesus as their Lord

Heaven: Jesus called it His Father's house. He is preparing a place with no pain, suffering, or tears for those who believe in Him.

Holy: To be separate for God

Lord: A master; the boss; someone who has power over another

Peace: No conflict; no fighting with God

Pray: To talk to God

Resurrection: The event when Jesus came back to life after being dead

Righteous: Right with God

The Golden Rule: What many people call this verse: "Do unto others as you would have them do unto you."

Tithe: A gift of thanksgiving given to God; equals one-tenth of earnings, but you can always give more

Works: The things you do

Scripture Memory Verses

Memorize the following verses. Use the chart to track your success.

If your child memorized any of these verses, I would love to know!

Please share your progress on the FutureFlyingSaucers Facebook page or contact me at futureflyingsaucers@klopex.com.

Verses	I can say it!
Romans 3:23	
Matthew 4:17	
Romans 10:9-10	
Acts 2:41	
John 15:14	
Matthew 22:37-38	
Matthew 6:33	
Matthew 6:9	
John 14:12	
Colossians 3:20	
Matthew 7:12	
John 13:34	
Matthew 5:44-46	
Matthew 18:21-22	

Verses	I can say it!
Matthew 9:37-38	
Matthew 28:19-20	
Matthew 4:4	
Luke 22:19-20	
Matthew 6:21	
Romans 5:1	
Hebrews 11:6	
Romans 8:9	
John 14:2	
Ephesians 2:6	
John 3:16	
1 John 5:12-13	
James 1:12	

Acknowledgements

Thank you to Pastor Josh Phillips for encouraging me to write this book.

Thank you to Emily Heinz for taking a chance with her old 4th grade teacher to create a resource for children.

Thank you to Stephanie Jackson who has become my right arm in online ministry and my friend.

How to Lead a Child to Christ

Salvation is a big deal and you don't want a child to decide what she really doesn't mean or understand. If at any point you sense that there is confusion or uncertainty on the child's part, say, *"I can tell that God is working in your heart. I want you to keep listening and learning."*

Ask many questions because you want the child to have to think through what they are doing. These questions should not be answered by "Yes," "No," or "Jesus." Use lots of scripture because you want God's word to be working.

At this point lead the child in prayer and have the child copy, or you can tell the child what information should be included when asking God for salvation:

- Admit to God you are a sinner.
- Say that you are sorry for those sins. Ask for forgiveness.
- Tell Jesus you believe Jesus is God's Son and that He died on the cross and rose again.
- Confess that Jesus is your Lord and Master.
- Thank God for saving you.

Once the child has prayed, read Hebrews 13:5b and 6a. Ask, *What has Jesus done for you?* This will give assurance of salvation.

Examples of Counseling Questions

1. Why have you decided to talk with me?
2. Why do you need Jesus as your Savior?
3. What is sin?
4. What are some examples of sin?
5. Can you do anything to get rid of sin?
6. Read Romans 3:23.
7. Who is Jesus?
8. What did Jesus do for you?
9. Read 1 Corinthians 15:3-4.
10. Read John 3:16 or Acts 16:31.
11. Would you like to pray to God and receive Jesus now?

Other Books by Anne Marie Gosnell

**Flexible, Multi-Age,
Budget Friendly Bible Lessons**

Because time is short.
Classroom Chaos is no fun.
Teach intentionally.

I help busy parents and church leaders teach fun, flexible, multi-age, budget-friendly bible object lessons that enhance the spiritual growth of children.

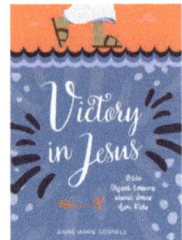

www.ingramcontent.com/pod-product-compliance
Lightning Source LLC
Chambersburg PA
CBHW051553010526
44118CB00022B/2692